What Is God's Will for My Life?

WHAT IS
GOD'S WILL
FOR
MY LIFE?

?

JOHN ORTBERG

Tyndale House Publishers, Inc.
Carol Stream, Illinois

Visit Tyndale online at www.tyndale.com.

TYNDALE and Tyndale's quill logo are registered trademarks of Tyndale House Publishers, Inc.

What Is God's Will for My Life?

Designed by Jacqueline L. Nuñez

Edited by Jonathan Schindler

Published in association with Yates & Yates (www.yates2.com).

ISBN 978-1-4964-1564-6

Printed in the United States of America

22	21	20	19	18	17	16
7	6	5	4	3	2	

FINDING GOD'S WILL FOR YOUR LIFE

THIS BOOK IS FOR YOU—the one who decides.

Whether your decisions look large or small. Whether you are running a large company or are all by yourself. Our decisions are our lives.

If you have ever been uncertain about what to do.

If you've ever prayed for wisdom but still didn't know which road to choose.

If you've ever been awake late at night because a past decision haunted you and you wished you could take it back.

If you've ever been so frustrated that you were tempted to flip a coin just to get the decision behind you.

If you've ever made a rash decision in a short time and lived to regret it for a long time.

If you've ever procrastinated on a decision and lost an opportunity.

If you've ever come to doubt your ability to choose wisely at all.

If you've ever wondered where God is in all this; if you've ever been afraid you were missing signals from heaven; if you've ever wondered whether you're proceeding from fleshly presumption or divine guidance; if you've ever felt the pressure that you might be choosing less than God's best for your life—

This book is for you.

WHAT IS GOD'S WILL FOR MY LIFE?

"'FOR I KNOW THE PLANS I have for you,' declares the LORD, 'plans to prosper you and not to harm you, plans to give you hope and a future'" (Jeremiah 29:11).

What an amazing thought. Those words first came to the people of Israel through the prophet Jeremiah when they were suffering in exile and all their plans had gone unfulfilled and it seemed as though they had no hope at all.

But that promise doesn't only relate to them. For thousands of years millions of people have been encouraged by the thought that the God of the universe cares about them. And the writers of Scripture say not only that God has a plan or a "will" for us, but that we can come to know it. The apostle Paul wrote, "Do not conform to the pattern of this world, but be transformed by the renewing of your mind. Then you will be able to test and approve what God's will is—his good, pleasing and perfect will" (Romans 12:2).

So God has a will for your life, it's good (and pleasing and perfect!), and you can come to know it.

And yet for many people the thought of God's will raises troubling questions even as it provides encouragement.

If God has a will for my life, why does it often seem so difficult to discover? How specific is it? Does God have one person for me to marry, or one job for me to take, or one place for me to live? What happens if I choose something that wasn't God's will for my life—am I stuck with less than God's best for my future? Why is it that some people seem to have so much more clarity than I do about God's will? How do I know for sure whether a choice is really God's will for me or just something I want to do?

This is not simply an abstract question that theologians wrestle over. If I get details about the end times wrong, I can still lead the right life. But one of the weightiest aspects of human life is *I must choose.* And my choices create my life. My choices create my destiny. I don't want to miss that!

Maybe you're facing graduation. More than anything else, young adults want to work at a job that inspires them, that has meaning. Maybe your prayer is *God, I don't want to choose mostly based on money or security or reputation. Help me find a calling that is worth my life.*

Maybe you're in a relationship, and you're confused about the next step. You always thought that when you found your soul mate, you would "just know." Yet now you just *don't* know. What if you marry this person and then meet your *real* soul mate at the reception?

Maybe you're in transition. People are changing jobs, companies, and whole careers more often than ever before. Career specialist Andy Chan notes that young adults will hold on average twenty-nine jobs over the course of their lives. Oxford researchers predict that over the next two decades about half the jobs that exist today will be replaced by technology.[1] How do you adapt to a changing environment? How do you weigh the options well?

Maybe you're in a rut. Your life is safe, but it's not fulfilling. There is something gnawing inside of you, the call of the open door.

Maybe you're facing an empty nest. You have freedom and time and possibilities that have not been available for decades, but you're not sure what to do with them.

Maybe you're retiring, but you know the

word *retire* is not in the Bible, and you're not ready for death or shuffleboard. What might God have for you next?

Maybe you have a great passion for a cause. You've seen a great need that just gnaws at you, or you studied a problem and want to make a difference. What's the next step? Whom do you talk to?

Maybe you're a student trying to decide which school to go to or which major to choose.

Maybe you're on the brink of an exciting adventure. Maybe you've been frustrated by a lost opportunity, and you wonder, *Does God still have another one for me?*

Your life is about more than safety. It's about more than security. It's about more than manageability. If you're looking for that stuff, you were born into the wrong species.

God has a plan for you. But that doesn't mean God wants to make all your decisions for you. This leads to one of the most gnawing questions about the will of God.

If God's will for my life is so important, why doesn't he tell me what it is more plainly?

Often we pray most fervently to know God's will when we're facing our biggest decisions. Which school should I attend? Which major should I choose? Whom should I marry? Where should I live? Which job should I choose?

Often we are frustrated when, in spite of our fervent prayers, heaven seems silent on these subjects. We feel like either we are praying the wrong prayers or God isn't living up to his end of the bargain. Even when we sincerely want to know what his will is, we may not get an answer.

But if you have ever faced a major decision, prayed, and not received clear "guidance," there may well be a good reason:

God's primary will for your life is not the circumstances you inhabit; it's the person you become.

God's primary will for your life is not what job you ought to take. It's not primarily situational or circumstantial. It's not mainly the city where you live or whether you get married or what house you ought to be in. God's primary will for your life is that you become a magnificent person in his image, somebody with the character of Jesus. That is God's main will for your life. No circumstance can prevent that.

This is why passages in the Bible about God's will for us consistently talk about the kind of person we're becoming:

- "For this is the will of God, that by doing good you should put to silence the ignorance of foolish people." (1 Peter 2:15, ESV)
- "Rejoice always, pray continually, give thanks in all circumstances; for this is God's will for you in Christ Jesus." (1 Thessalonians 5:16-18)

- "It is God's will that you should be sanctified." (1 Thessalonians 4:3)
- "We continually ask God to fill you with the knowledge of his will through all the wisdom and understanding that the Spirit gives, so that you may live a life worthy of the Lord." (Colossians 1:9-10)
- "Be very careful, then, how you live— not as unwise but as wise. . . . Do not be foolish, but understand what the Lord's will is." (Ephesians 5:15-17)

But this truth about the nature of God's will for us has a crucial implication: God's will for us is that we become persons of excellent character—and one of the primary tools for building excellent character is decision making. If people never go through the challenge and anxiety and responsibility of decision making, their growth will be stunted.

We all understand that, especially parents.

If you're a parent, would you want the kind of kids you have to tell their whole lives, "Wear these clothes. Take these classes. Go to that school. Apply for this job. Marry that person. Purchase this house," and who always do exactly what you tell them as long as they live?

"No" is the correct answer here. No, you wouldn't want that.

Why? Because your main goal is not for them to be little robots that carry out instructions. Your goal is that they become people of great character and judgment. The only way for them to do that is to make lots and lots of decisions. Of course, that means they'll make a lot of wrong decisions. That becomes a primary way they learn.

Very often God's will for you will be "I want you to decide" because decision making is an indispensable part of character formation. God is primarily in the character-forming business, not the circumstance-shaping business.

This means a new way of looking at life. I

do not have to be afraid of failure. I do not have to live in fear over circumstances. Each moment is an opportunity to look for a door that opens up into God and his presence.

This means a new way of looking at myself. I am no longer limited by my smallness and weakness. The God who wants me to "grow up in all things into Him who is the head—Christ" (Ephesians 4:15, NKJV) is also the God who knows how small and weak I am.

This means a new way of looking at decisions. I no longer have to live under the tyranny of the perfect choice. God can use even what looks like the "wrong choice" if I make it with the right heart. Years ago a movie called *The Stepford Wives* told about women who were replaced by identical-looking robots. They were (at least from their chauvinistic husbands' point of view) perfect in their practice of carrying out their "duties"—always happy, always lovely, always sweet. They just weren't *people*.

God is not interested in making Stepford Christians. God is perfectly capable of creating robots, but you won't find any in Genesis. God's will for your life includes his intention that you exercise initiative and creativity and curiosity and that you learn to accept responsibility with grace and poise. This is all part of what God expressed when he created human beings in his own image and told them to "have dominion" (Genesis 1:26, 28, KJV). God's will for your life includes his desire that *you* should have a will!

In other words, God's basic will for your life is not what you do or where you live or whether you marry or how much you make. It's who you become. God's primary will for your life is that you become a person of excellent character, wholesome liveliness, and divine love.

If parents' desire is for their children to become truly good people, they will often *insist* that their children make their own decisions.

Persons of excellent will, judgment, and character get formed no other way.

This means that God's will for your life will often be "You decide." Sometimes you will ask heaven for direction, and God will say, "I don't care which option you choose." That doesn't mean God doesn't care about *you*. It means that God cares more about your personhood and character than anything else—which is of course what we would expect from a truly loving God.

Sometimes God may have a specific assignment for someone—like Moses confronting Pharaoh, or Jonah going to Nineveh, or Paul preaching to the Gentiles—and God is perfectly competent to make this clear. And wisdom itself will help us know the right course in many choices.

But it is a tremendous help to faith and prayer to realize that a lack of guidance from heaven around which choice to make does not mean either God or you have failed. Very often it is just the opposite—God knows you will grow more from having to make a decision than from getting a memo from heaven that will prevent you from growing.

There are so many options— how do I choose?

We are decision makers. Our lives are a series of choices. This is true more in our day than ever before. People used to enter arranged marriages—now we decide whether we'll marry and whom. Boys used to enter their father's profession, and girls grew up to be homemakers; now we must decide what we'll do. Throughout history people generally lived and died in the village where they were born; now we must choose where to live. People used to follow their tribal religion; now we must choose what we'll believe.

We face what one researcher calls choice fatigue.

Columbia researcher Sheena Iyengar has found that the average person makes about seventy conscious decisions every day.[2] That's 25,550 decisions a year. Over seventy years, that's 1,788,500 decisions. Albert Camus said, "Life is a sum of all your choices." You put all those 1,788,500 choices together, and that's who you are.

Sometimes when I desperately want "God's will," what I *really* want isn't God's will at all. What I really want is what I want. Or it's to off-load the anxiety of decision making.

Princeton philosopher Walter Kaufmann coined the word *decidophobia*. He noticed that human beings are afraid of making decisions. We don't want the anxiety that accompanies the possibility of being wrong. Decisions wear us out.

Decision making creates stress and anxiety. Therefore, we're not just decision makers; we're also mistake avoiders.

We know that a wrong decision can ruin

our lives. We know from watching others, and we ourselves have experienced what happens when we choose the wrong friends or the wrong job or the wrong marriage or the wrong behaviors.

We prize the freedom to choose, but we dread the mistakes that can wreck our lives. And we dislike the pressure of responsibility.

So people have always looked for help beyond themselves in making decisions. Sometimes this has involved resorting to magic—reading tea leaves or the stars or crystal balls or palms. Writers of Scripture always strongly warned against these practices because they are an attempt to leverage the supernatural without concern for justice or goodness or character.

Other times people meet with professional counselors or use assessment tools to help with career choices, or they consult dating services to find a spouse. People ask friends for advice. People flip coins.

People of faith want to know about God's will for their lives. If there is an all-knowing and deeply loving God, it only makes sense to turn to him first in the valley of decision because if I violate God's will for my life, I am cutting against the grain of the Maker of the universe.

What matters most is not just God's will for *my* life, but God's will and purpose for his cosmic project of creation—what might be called his Great Will. His Great Will is to create a redeemed community of loving persons who are continually creating value in joyful partnership with him. That's something all of us can participate in.

If my circumstances seem to take a wrong turn, does that mean I missed God's will?

When God was taking Israel to Canaan during the Exodus, it seemed like it would be a very simple journey. He said he was going to take them out of a bad place (slavery and Egypt) and to a good place (the Promised Land, flowing with milk and honey).

This involved a short walk across the Sinai Peninsula. It could be done in a week. But none of them could have imagined what would happen next.

The text explains what God was up to:

When Pharaoh let the people go, God did not lead them on the road through the Philistine country, though that was shorter. For God said, "If they face war, they might change their minds and return to Egypt." So God led the people around by the desert road toward the Red Sea. (Exodus 13:17-18)

The Common English Bible uses a wonderful phrase to describe this. It says God led them on "the roundabout way."

Imagine the people's surprise when the pillar of cloud God sent turns south instead of northeast, where they know they're supposed to go. The pillar is directionally challenged.

But to God, *who* they are is more important than *where* they are. And who they are is easily discouraged, lacking in faith, and viewing themselves as slaves who are without power.

It took one day to get them out of Egypt. It took forty years to get the Egypt out of them.

So they were led into the wilderness. The wilderness is the place no one wants to go.

Maybe for you it's a wilderness of depression. Maybe it's a wilderness of loneliness. Maybe it's a wilderness of failure. Maybe it's a wilderness of doubt.

The wilderness is not just a place of disappointment. It's also the furnace of transformation.

It's worth noting, too, that nobody in Israel

knew they'd be spending forty years on the roundabout way. It's the nature of life that we never know exactly what it is we're getting into.

When we have big choices to make—taking a job, making a move, getting into a relationship, having a baby—we all want to know ahead of time, "What exactly are we getting into?"

Yet we never know.

And that's a very good thing, because a lot of times if we knew what we were getting into, we wouldn't get into it in the first place. Frederick Buechner says, "God's coming is always unforeseen, I think, and the reason, if I had to guess, is that if he gave us anything much in the way of advance warning, more often than not we would have made ourselves scarce long before he got there."[3]

In the Bible, when God calls someone to do something, no one responds by saying, "I'm ready":

- Moses: "I have never been eloquent
  . . . I am slow of speech and tongue."
  (Exodus 4:10)
- Gideon: "How can I save Israel? My clan
  is the weakest in Manasseh, and I am the
  least in my family." (Judges 6:15)
- Abraham: "Will a son be born to a
  man a hundred years old?" (Genesis
  17:17)
- Jeremiah: "Alas, Sovereign LORD, . . .
  I am too young." (Jeremiah 1:6)
- Isaiah: "Woe to me! . . . For I am a
  man of unclean lips." (Isaiah 6:5)
- Esther: "For any man or woman who
  approaches the king . . . without being
  summoned the king has but one law:
  . . . death." (Esther 4:11)
- Rich Young Ruler: "He went away
  sad, because he had great wealth."
  (Matthew 19:22)
- Ruth: "There was a famine in the
  land." (Ruth 1:1)

- Saul (Samuel was going to anoint Saul king; they couldn't find him and asked if he was present.): "And the LORD said, 'Yes, he has hidden himself among the supplies.'" (1 Samuel 10:22)

Too inarticulate, too weak, too old, too young, too sinful, too dangerous, too rich, too poor, too much baggage—no one *ever* says, "Okay, Lord—I feel *ready*." And God says to us what he has always said: "Ready or not . . ."

Feeling ready is highly overrated. God isn't looking for readiness; he's looking for obedience. When God brought the people of Israel into the Promised Land, he had them step into the Jordan first, *then* he parted the river. If they had waited for proof, they'd be standing on the banks still.

Pastor Craig Groeschel put God's determination to use us like this: "If you're not dead, you're not done."

Abraham was seventy-five years old when God promised him a son. He had to wait an additional twenty-four years. He made numerous wrong choices. He lied and said that Sarah was his sister rather than his wife (twice!). He slept with Sarah's servant when it seemed like God was never going to act.

When God repeated his promise, "Abraham fell facedown; he laughed and said to himself, 'Will a son be born to a man a hundred years old? Will Sarah bear a child at the age of ninety?'" (Genesis 17:17).

"Sarah will bear you a son," God responded (Genesis 17:19). "I don't care how old she is." If you're not dead, you're not done.

Abraham tries to say no because he's too old. Timothy tries to say no because he's too young. Esther tries to say no because she's the wrong gender. Moses tries to say no because he has the wrong gifts. Gideon tries to say no because he's from the wrong tribe. Elijah tries to say no because he has the wrong enemy.

Jonah tries to say no because he's being sent to the wrong city. Paul tries to say no because he has the wrong background. God keeps saying, "Go, go. *You* go." Sometimes it takes a while for God's promises to be fulfilled. But if you're not dead, that's the clue you're not done.

Moses chose murder. David chose murder and adultery and a cover-up. Gideon chose fear. Samson chose Delilah. Elijah chose to run away from Jezebel. Jonah chose a watery escape. Peter chose to lop off a soldier's ear.

And yet all of them are in the book. God isn't in the business of rejecting people who make wrong choices; he's in the business of redeeming them. If only people who made correct choices were used by God, the Bible would be a much shorter book, and Jesus would be the only character.

The real question isn't about *if* I make a wrong decision; it's about *when* I make a wrong decision. And the answer is that as soon as I surrender my will, God will recalculate my route and welcome me home.

If you're not dead, you're not done.

Will God be angry at me or punish me if I make a bad choice?

God is not mad at you.

In ancient times, people used to have to find guidance for road trips through something called "maps." Now we have a GPS or Google or Siri. Now we have a voice to give us directions.

We still sometimes get lost. It might be that we're not paying attention and miss a turn. Or perhaps we don't trust the directions, and we go left when we were instructed to go right.

In that case, once we know we're lost and are ready to listen to direction, we'll always receive the same message: "Recalculating route. When able, execute a U-turn."

The guidance system is always quite patient with us. The voice will never say, "You little twerp. Why didn't you listen to me? I told you so." It will never say, "You think you're so smart. Go ahead and find your own way now." It will never say, "Because you chose the wrong route, you will never be allowed to get to your true destination."

Why would we think that God is less patient or less loving than a GPS?

Jesus told many stories about people who made wrong choices. One is about a character who has become known as the Prodigal Son. He chooses to leave his home, waste his inheritance, and dishonor his father. But when he comes to his senses, he is ready for guidance. "Recalculating route. Execute a U-turn."

He assumes that he'll be stuck with plan B for the rest of his life—"I don't deserve to be treated like a son anymore; I'll just live from now on as a hired hand"—but his father has no intention of letting him settle for a plan B.

All of our choices have consequences. For the Prodigal Son, he will never have the time he spent wallowing with pigs back. But that doesn't mean he's stuck with plan B. He just has a new plan A. God specializes in improvisation. He loves to throw parties for prodigals who come home.

Sometimes we may make a choice in good faith, and it just turns out badly. We take a job at a company that goes bankrupt or buy a car that turns out to be a lemon. We may feel foolish or guilty, but God doesn't expect anybody but him to be omniscient. The psalmist says that God "remembers that we are dust" (Psalm 103:14). And dust—even relatively educated dust—is pretty fallible when it comes to choosing.

Sometimes I may actually know what God wants me to do and refuse to do it. Or I may know that God wants me *not* to do something, and I do it anyway. This is more complicated than a wrong choice made simply from ignorance. So let's look at the patron saint of those who resist God's will—a prophet named Jonah.

The word of the Lord comes to Jonah: "Go to the great city of Nineveh and preach against it, because its wickedness has come up before me" (Jonah 1:2).

Jonah, rather than obeying God, runs away. But God is persistent. He sends a storm so that Jonah is thrown overboard and then sends a whale so that Jonah will turn to him.

So Jonah goes to Nineveh when it is clear the alternative is to become a living sushi bar. He preaches a message, but his message may be the lamest in all the Bible: "Forty more days and Nineveh will be overthrown" (Jonah 3:4).

Jonah preaches what may be the worst sermon of all time. No mention of God or repentance or mercy. No illustration, no application, no edification. Jonah is putting no effort into this at all. He's phoning it in.

But the strangest thing happens. People listen. They begin to respond. Their response is so widespread that everyone from the king all the way down to the poorest and weakest citizen repents, and even the animals wear sackcloth.

God sees Nineveh's repentance and is filled with compassion. "When God saw what they did and how they turned from their evil ways, he relented" (Jonah 3:10).

Jonah looks at all this, and you would think he'd be thrilled.

"But to Jonah this seemed very wrong, and he became angry" (Jonah 4:1).

At the end of the book, God is still pleading with Jonah to stop pouting. We're not told how Jonah responded, because this is one of those stories where *we're* supposed to respond. But we come to understand that God hasn't given up on old Jonah yet. And God hasn't given up on you or me, either. What will *I* do? Whose will will *I* choose?

It remains an open question, even when I've made a bad choice.

How can I know if what I'm doing is going *against* God's will? Is there some kind of litmus test?

Paul writes that when we "do not conform to the pattern of this world" but are "transformed by the renewing of [our] mind," we will "be able to test and approve what God's will is" (Romans 12:2). Here are several guideposts to help you do that.

JESUS' TEACHINGS

The first and most important question that can guide us is, Is this decision in line with Jesus' teachings about life, or is it incompatible with what he says about true inner goodness? Jesus once asked, "Why do you call me, 'Lord, Lord,' and do not do what I say?" (Luke 6:46).

Jesus' primary concern is always not behavioral compliance to some rule but the condition of our inner selves. His general summary can sound pretty intimidating: "Be perfect, . . . as your heavenly Father is perfect" (Matthew 5:48). But he doesn't say, "Be a perfectionist." His will for us is that we grow toward more perfect love and forgiveness and fidelity and truthfulness.

One reason it's important to become a student of Jesus and to immerse ourselves in his teaching is that it's so tempting to rationalize what we want to do by staying vague. "I know God's will is for me to be happy, and in order to be happy, I know that I must have X; therefore, it must be God's will for me to have X."

Sociologist Christian Smith says the fastest-growing religion in America is "Moralistic Therapeutic Deism." This is an approach to spiritual life that involves the notion that God wants everybody to be nice, that God is especially concerned that I be happy, and that God is a fairly remote being about whom I don't think much unless I hit a crisis.

But Jesus had matchless clarity about what goodness consists of, and his teachings are worth submitting my decisions to:

- Is this decision congruent with the reality that "it is more blessed to give than to receive" (Acts 20:35)?
- Will this decision help me "not worry about [my] life" (Matthew 6:25) but trust my heavenly Father?
- Is this decision compatible with sexual integrity so that I am both avoiding sexual wrongdoing (sexual intimacy outside marriage) as well as not indulging lust in my inner person?
- Will this decision enable me to follow the Golden Rule?
- Will this decision help me to love my neighbor?

YOUR SPIRITUAL GIFTS

The Bible teaches that everybody who follows Jesus has received gifts from the Holy Spirit. Understanding and embracing the unique ways God has wired you is an indispensable part of discovering God's will for your life. Perhaps you are someone who loves to offer hospitality, or you are a born encourager, or administration comes naturally to you, or you have found yourself pursuing leadership activities since grade school.

You have discovered a critical piece of God's road map for your life. Making decisions that are in line with the exercise of your spiritual gifts will honor God and bring you joy.

SUSTAINABILITY

Increasingly, we live in a world of exhausted people. But chronic exhaustion is not God's will for us. Jesus says, "Come to me, all you who are weary and burdened, and I will give you rest. Take my yoke upon you and learn from me, for I am gentle and humble in heart, and you will find rest for your souls. For my yoke is easy and my burden is light" (Matthew 11:28-30).

One criterion to keep in mind when making a decision is what might be called the "Jethro test." During the Exodus, Moses had taken on the task of giving guidance to the entire nation of Israel. That meant he had an endless stream of people asking him to render decisions about their problems and conflicts. Decision making takes energy, and Moses was depleted.

So his father-in-law, Jethro, advised him, "What you are doing is not good. You and these people who come to you will only wear yourselves out. The work is too heavy for you; you cannot handle it alone" (Exodus 18:17-18). He counseled Moses to be in constant prayer ("bring their disputes to [God]"), to teach people about spiritual wisdom, and then to appoint wise leaders to guide people in smaller groups.

God used Jethro to help guide Moses even though Jethro had been a "priest of Midian" (Exodus 18:1)—not even a member of God's people. Getting counsel from wise people is always helpful—and God can use anyone to guide you.

SPIRITUAL DISCERNMENT

In Scripture we are commanded to "test the spirits" (1 John 4:1), and one concrete way to do this is associated with Ignatius of Loyola. He had been a soldier who was hungry for glory on the battlefield and quite vain about his own appearance (he once had his leg rebroken to make it look more attractive!). After being injured in battle, he had a long convalescence and began to wonder what God's will might be for his future. He was torn between two options—to continue to be a soldier or to give up military life and devote himself to acts of service and prayer.

Imagining himself doing either of these gave

him pleasure, but he found that when he pictured himself as a successful soldier, his sense of pleasure would fade away. It had a kind of unpleasant emotional aftertaste. However, when he imagined himself engaged in a life of servanthood and study, his initial joy lingered.

This has become an important process in Christian decision making. The idea is that when I'm facing an important choice in any area, I seek to be open to all alternatives. I consider each possibility deeply. I ask myself the question, *Will this move me closer to God or farther away? Is it congruent with becoming the person I believe God created me to be?*

On the other hand, sometimes people use criteria that are less than helpful to discern God's will.

A FALSE METHOD: THE ALLURE OF "PEACE" AND "EASY"

Recognizing the angst of difficult decision making can help you avoid one of the worst, overspiritualized traps people fall into when faced with a daunting opportunity: the "I just don't feel peace about it" excuse for ca-pitulating to fear or laziness. In this scenario, we take the presence of internal anxiety as a supernatural rationale for avoiding a chal-lenge rather than seeing it for what it is—a simple sign of emotional immaturity.

"Why don't you end that relationship in which you're behaving like a needy, desper-ate, clinging vine with a person who's just not that into you?"

"Why don't you have an honest conversation with that person in your workplace/family/ small group who is behaving badly and whom you are secretly judging and resenting?"

"Why don't you get out of your rut by taking this trip or that class or volunteering in these areas?"

"Well, I would, but I just don't have peace about it."

If "having peace about it" were the ultimate

criterion for testing God's will, nobody in the Bible would have done anything God asked. The sequence in the Bible is usually not:

- Calling
- Deep Feeling of Peace about It
- Decision to Obey
- Smooth Sailing

Instead, it's usually:

- Calling
- Abject Terror
- Decision to Obey
- Big Problems
- More Terror
- Second Thoughts
- Repeat Several Times
- Deeper Faith

Once we've made a difficult decision, we often experience anxiety and second thoughts. Having second thoughts about a choice we've made is not unusual. It's not an automatic sign we've made the wrong choice. It's not even a good predictor of the future. Israel fluctuated in how they felt about the decision to leave Egypt through the Red Sea. One moment they were terrified ("Defy Pharoah? I don't think so!"). The next, elated ("The Red Sea has parted!"). Then the decision looked awful ("Manna again?"), then wonderful ("Get Daddy's shotgun—look at those quail!").

Following God's will does not mean life will be easy on the other side. So often we romanticize the opportunities God presents us with, and we think, *Man, if God just opens the door for me, it will all be success, glory, ease, joy . . .* Think about this. Of course God opens doors for people all through the Bible. From Abraham on, it's just this story of God calling one person after another.

But when in the Bible does God ever give

anybody an easy job? When does God ever call somebody, set before them an open door, and say to them, "This won't inconvenience you much. You can polish this task off in a couple of minutes. I don't really want it to be a burden on you"? Never. God never says it will be easy. What he does say is "I will go with you."

God comes to Noah. He says, "I want you to leave everything. I want you to build an ark. You're going to face ridicule and hostility. You're going to face judgment. You're going to face a decimated planet. You're going to face a flood, but I will be with you, Noah, and I'll give you a sign—a rainbow. Every time you see that rainbow, you'll know you're not alone."

Noah says, "Wow. I'll go."

God comes to Abraham and says, "I want you to leave everything familiar—your home, your culture, your safety, your security, your language. I want you to go to a place I will show you, but I will be with you, and I will give you a sign that I will be with you. It's called circumcision."

And Abraham says, "Noah got a rainbow. Couldn't it be, like, a secret handshake or a decoder ring or something like that?"

God never says it's going to be easy, but sometimes people will deceive themselves that they are being "spiritual" when they are really doing anxiety management: "I just don't feel peace about it." When in the Bible does God ever tell someone like Moses, "Go to Pharaoh," or David, "Face Goliath," or Daniel, "Go into a lion's den," or Esther, "Face Haman," and have somebody say, "Yes, Lord. I feel peace about that"? Peace lies on the other side of obedience, on the other side of the door, not this side. Peace does not lie in getting God to give me other circumstances. Peace lies in finding God in *these* circumstances.

While we're visiting these heroes of the Bible, it's a good moment to reflect. If you're facing something really hard—something hard in ministry, something hard in volunteering, a challenge, discouragement, not having the results you wanted—you are not alone. You are not the first person in the history of God's mission to have a hard assignment. Just know you're not at the end of your story yet.

"I've got a peaceful easy feeling" is an Eagles song, not a Bible verse.

ONE LAST TEST

God gave us our wills and is delighted that we have them. But our wills have very little power on their own. *Our wills were made to surrender to God.*

This is why in twelve-step programs there is a strength in will-surrender ("made a decision to turn our will and our lives over to the care of God as we understood him") that is greater than the strength of willpower. So there is a last question we can ask to help in our discernment: Am I willing or willful?

We might think of the difference between an open hand and a clenched fist.

Any parent of a two-year-old understands what willfulness looks like. I insist on having my way. I throw a tantrum (at least inside) if my will is frustrated. I make an idol of my own desires. I clutch and cling. I clench my little fists.

But if I am willing, I have open hands before God. Palms up. I'm aware of my desires but ready to surrender them if need be. I have taken ego off the throne. I have resigned from the office of "God for a Day."

"Not my will, but yours be done."

What spiritual disciplines can I begin practicing to grow in decision making and discernment?

1. PRAYER

Prayer is to our spirits what breathing is to our bodies. It connects us to our lifelines. Prayer is "talking with God about what we're doing together."[4] Decision time is prayer time.

James writes, "If any of you lacks wisdom, you should ask God, who gives generously to all without finding fault" (James 1:5). It's significant that in this passage James talks about how we develop as persons—how difficulties can help us grow stronger character. Difficulties always require decision. James does not counsel us to try to off-load the decision. He encourages us to ask not for *directions* but for *wisdom*. Prayer is the single most important discipline for growth in this area because it allows us to share the burden with God and still grow in our wisdom at the same time.

Choosing comes from the core of who we are. When we truly choose, we have no one to blame and nowhere to hide. Choosing thrills us. Choosing scares us. Choosing is central to personhood. Poet Archibald MacLeish has said, "What is freedom? Freedom is the right to choose: the right to create for oneself the alternatives of choice. Without the possibility of choice a man is not a man but a member, an instrument, a thing."[5]

God wants us to learn to choose well. That may be why, when we look at the Bible, there is no chapter devoted to "How to Know God's Will for Your Life." Often when we are faced with a real-life choice, the Bible seems no more helpful than Yogi Berra's old dictum, "When you come to a fork in the road, take it." Paul doesn't write about "Six Steps to Determine If He's the One" or "Five Ways to Discern God's Job for You."

What we do see are statements like the passage from James above. Or "This is my prayer: that your love may abound more and more in knowledge and depth of insight, so that you may be able to discern what is best" (Philippians 1:9-10).

God wants us to be excellent choosers.

Another poet, Dr. Seuss, says, "Simple

it's not, I'm afraid you will find, for a mind-maker-upper to make up his mind."[6] And God is growing mind-maker-uppers, not just order-carry-outers.

If we're facing a choice and want to find God's will for our lives, we shouldn't begin by asking which choice is God's will for our lives. We need to begin by asking for wisdom.

We must pray and then proceed with the conscious assumption that God will answer. Based on that assumption, we begin looking around to see if perhaps he has answered in a way we might otherwise have missed.

A woman locked her keys in her car in a rough neighborhood. She tried using a coat hanger to break into her car, but she couldn't get that to work. Finally, she prayed, "God, send me somebody to help me." Five minutes later, a rusty old car pulled up. A tattooed, bearded man wearing a biker's skull rag walked toward her. She thought, *God, really? Him?* But she was desperate.

So when the man asked if he could help, she said, "Can you break into my car?"

He said, "Not a problem." He took the coat hanger and opened the car in a few seconds.

She said to him, "You're a very nice man" and gave him a big hug.

He said, "I'm not a nice man. I just got out of prison today. I served two years for auto theft, and I've only been out a couple of hours."

She hugged him again and shouted, "Thank you, God, for sending me a professional!"

It's a wonderful gift to be able to ask God for guidance. But it's necessary to talk to God about other things as well: to give him worship, to express gratitude, to seek learning, to draw hope.

In fact, this leads to a critical dynamic about seeking God's will for my life: guidance is only one part of a full relationship with God.

(Similar to any friendship—if the only time I communicate with you is to get direction/information that is useful to me, we will not have much of a relationship.) It only makes sense for God to give me guidance if I'm in a deeper relationship with him that is forming my character and heart.

I will never experience guidance from God if my main goal with God is to get guidance.

A full relationship with God will include intimacy, confession, worship, gratitude, learning, receiving encouragement, and surrender. These are all elements needed for me to become the kind of person God can use to achieve his good and great will. The critical question when it comes to guidance is not "Is God willing to give guidance?" It's "Am I becoming the kind of person it makes sense for God to give guidance to?" When I am selfish or greedy or resentful, any knowledge I might gain about the future would simply enable me to do more harm.

2. REST

One of the main reasons why "finding God's will for my life" is such a huge topic in our day is that we are overwhelmed by the sheer volume of choices we must make.

Barry Schwartz said his local grocery store offers 285 kinds of cookies and 175 brands of salad dressing. The menu at Cheesecake Factory is longer than *War and Peace*. The beauty of blue jeans used to be their simplicity—they were blue, and they were jeans. Now you have to choose: boot cut, relaxed fit (what a gentle way of putting it), skinny jeans, distressed jeans (for pants that match your mood), acid washed, stone washed, pre-worn, bell bottom, straight cut, button fly, zipper fly, digital fly, beltless, and unileg. (I made that last one up.)

We do this because we think having more choices means more freedom, and more freedom means better living. But having too many choices does not produce liberation; it produces paralysis. In one study, the more options people were offered for investing their pension money, the *less* likely they were to invest. Even though their companies offered to *match* the amount of money they would invest in retirement, people left the money on the table.[7]

We have turned our world into a smorgasbord of choices, and it's starving us to death. We have become choiceaholics. And even the twelve steps can't help us, because it requires us to turn our will over to a Higher Power, and we don't have one more decision left in us.

Biblical characters didn't face this. Isaac didn't have to ask God whether Rebekah was "God's will for his life." He didn't have to decide which school to attend, and his career as an agrarian nomad was assigned at birth.

But there is wisdom for us from the ancient world. Good decision makers tend to simplify their lives so they can save their finite supply of willpower for the decisions that matter most. In monastic communities people don't have to waste energy deciding what they are going to wear on casual Friday. John the Baptist, Johnny Cash, and Steve Jobs always knew what they would be wearing, so they could save their mental energy for more important issues.

It turns out that choosing drains us. It takes energy. So wise people shepherd their "choosing energy" well.

In fact, one study found that the biggest factor influencing whether prisoners would get parole is whether their case came up before a judge early in the morning or late in the afternoon. Granting parole involves a certain risk, which requires energy, and judges (like most of us) tend to be fresher and better rested earlier in the day.

This is why wise people never make important decisions in a wrong emotional state. When Elijah found out Queen Jezebel was after him, he was ready to give up his prophet job and die. God gave him a giant time-out. Elijah took a nap, ate some food, took another nap, then had forty days of rest and prayer and recovery before he decided about what his next steps would be. He was now ready to decide on the basis of his faith and not his fear. And his decision was very different at the end of forty days of rest than it would have been before.

I have seen people make terrible decisions when they were drained, tired, discouraged, or afraid that they would never have made otherwise. Never try to choose the right course of action in the wrong frame of mind.

Wisdom may well have you wait to make a big decision until you're rested. An anxious mind and an exhausted body will lead to a terrible decision nine times out of ten.

3. SEEK COUNSEL

In Acts 13, we're told that a community of believers gathered together and devoted considerable time to prayer, worship, and fasting. Out of that experience we're told that "the Holy Spirit said, 'Set apart for me Barnabas and Saul for the work to which I have called them'" (verse 2). How did they know the Spirit said this? What did his voice sound like? The text doesn't say. Perhaps it was a dramatic moment; perhaps it was a leading they only clearly recognized to have been the Spirit afterward. (Often we see God's direction better through the rearview mirror than through the windshield.) But what is clear is they received guidance from God *together*, as a community.

On our own we are more vulnerable. Dan and Chip Heath call one error we make "narrow framing": we miss the full range of options God has before us because of our restricted thinking. We ask things like "Should I end this relationship or not?" instead of "How might I make this relationship better?" Or "Should I buy that or not?" rather than "What's the best way I can use this money?"[8]

We tend to suffer from "confirmation bias"—we seek out information that confirms what we already want rather than looking for the unvarnished truth. We pretend we want the truth—"What do you think of my tattoo? Do you like my girlfriend?"—but what we really want is reassurance of the positions we've already staked out.

This dynamic was well known in biblical times. Isaiah talked about people "who say to the seers, 'Do not see'; and to the prophets, 'Do not prophesy to us what is right; speak to us smooth things, prophesy illusions'" (Isaiah 30:10, NRSV).

We need others to help us choose wisely. But not just anyone. We need people with the wisdom to be discerning and the courage to be truthful.

Educator Parker Palmer writes about when he had to decide about taking a job as president of a college.[9] In the Quaker tradition, someone facing a major decision will often call together a "clearness committee," which seeks to discern God's will together. They do this not by waiting for someone to have a subjective feeling, nor by giving advice, but by asking probing questions. In Parker's case he could answer the questions easily for an hour until someone asked him what he would *like* about being president.

"Well, I would not like having to give up my writing and teaching. . . . I would not like the politics of the presidency. . . . I would not like having to glad-hand people I do not respect simply because they have money," he said.

"May I remind you that I asked what you would most *like*?"

"I would not like having to give up my summer vacations. . . . I would not like having to wear a suit and tie all the time."

"Parker, those are all things you would *dislike* about the job. What would you *like* about it?"

He got very quiet. "I guess what I'd like

most is getting my picture in the paper with the word *president* under it."

He decided not to take the job. But he would not have reached that decision on his own. Guidance often comes to us—as it came to Israel in the wilderness—through a relational context. Guidance is a team sport.

4. PRACTICE

Dr. Neil Warren has a wonderful exercise to develop your decision-making muscle. He talks about going into the "control room." This is a complement to seeking counsel, for here you own the responsibility of choosing. When you have a decision to make today (maybe it's a small one, like what to do with a free hour), you can practice this. Imagine a little room where only you can go. Your mother is not allowed in here, so you have to walk her out the door. Dad too. Nor is your spouse allowed, or your boss, or your therapist. Here you receive data from all important sources: from friends, from critics, from books, from emotional awareness, from experience. But then you silence all those voices. You surrender your ego to God. And then, asking God for help, you make the decision with full awareness and glad acceptance of responsibility.

One of the primary reasons for inauthenticity in our lives, Neil says, is that we do not exercise our God-given, God-powered ability to choose. We look to others for signals. We choose options that will please or placate or appease rather than doing the hard work of courageously and wisely owning our decisions before God.

The best way to learn how to make big decisions is to practice with lots of small ones. You might experiment with this for the next week or two:

- Whom do I want to talk to at work today?
- What shall I do with my free time tonight?

- What do I want to read today?
- What order shall I do my work in?
- What music would I enjoy listening to?
- Whom would I like to text?

Every conscious decision you make and own is a little push-up for your will. Over time, strength comes. God made us that way.

Afterward you take a few moments to review the outcome. In hindsight, was there any more information you should have gathered before you decided? Were you being driven by any emotions you weren't aware of? Decision making is a skill, like guitar playing or tightrope walking; you don't get better by just reading about it. You get better with diligent practice.

Is it okay to ask God for specific things that I want for my life?

It's always better to ask God for what we really want than to ask him for what we think we're supposed to want. Prayer dies when we pretend to be better than we are. Prayer is when we try to bring ourselves as we really are to God as he really is.

If we're asking for something that it would be unwise to grant, God will know that better than we will.

This is part of why it's such a good thing that prayer doesn't "work" in a mechanical way. In a "Peanuts" cartoon Linus tells his sister, "I think I've made a new theological discovery. If you hold your hands upside down, you get the opposite of what you pray for." We're always after some formula that would guarantee a prayer being granted.

It may be frustrating, but it's also wonderful that when we pray, God reserves the right to say no. All through the Bible we see negative responses to wrong requests. In fact, on four separate occasions, four different people—Moses, Jeremiah, Elijah, and Jonah—all ask God to take their lives. In every case God says, "No, no, no, no." Don't you think when their dark mood was past, they were glad God had said no?

Thank God he sometimes says no. There's a country song by Garth Brooks that hit number one on the charts some time ago called "Unanswered Prayers." He was at a football game at his old school, and he saw a girl he was nuts about when he was in school. He used to pray God would make that girl his wife. It didn't happen, and now all these years later, he sees her again and wonders, *What was I thinking?*

Under his breath, he whispers, "Thank God! Thank God!" The main line of the song is "Some of God's greatest gifts are unanswered prayers."

(Slightly sobering thought: you may be somebody's unanswered prayer.)

Should you pray for success in your work? Of course! Who would pray for failure? Sometimes in an effort to sound humble, people will attach a formula to their prayers: "I ask this only if it be thy will; if it's not thy will, don't do it." This caveat isn't really necessary. For one thing, since God is God, he knows his will is going to be done. For another, God is genuinely interested in your honestly asking him for what you want. If he's got something better to give you, he won't feel pressured into the wrong response. God has very little need for approval.

What's more, God himself knows the agony of closed doors—more than any human being ever will. God has given to every human being the key to the door of their own heart, and God himself will not force his way in. Jesus says, "Behold, I stand at the door and knock . . ." (Revelation 3:20, NKJV). It's not just we who hope God will open a door for *us*; God hopes *we* will open a door for *him*.

So we stand with him in our pain at the closed door.

I got a letter from the father of an eight-year-old daughter who had been diagnosed with a life-threatening and debilitating disease. He wrote, "Every day I pray for her healing. Every day I pray to understand. Every day I ask God, 'God, would you make me sick instead of my little girl? Let me suffer.' I'm so mad at God. I'm trying to hang on, but I'm so mad. Why is heaven silent on the one prayer I most want answered?"

You have been there too, or someplace like it. Or you will be sometime. I cannot point you to an explanation that has all the answers because nobody has all the answers. I can only point you to a Person. I can only tell you that at the heart of the gospel is an unanswered prayer. Jesus, kneeling in the garden, prayed, "Father, if it is possible, may this cup, this suffering, this death be taken from me. Yet not my will, but yours be done."

This is the most desperate prayer ever prayed from the most discerning spirit that ever lived, from the purest heart that ever beat, for deliverance from the most unjust suffering ever known. And all it got was silence. Heaven was not moved. The cup was not taken from him. The request was denied. The door remained closed.

From that unwanted, unmerited suffering came the hope of the world that remade history. Because the ultimate answer to every human anguish, including the anguish of unanswered prayer, is a sin-stained, blood-soaked cross where God himself suffered. Nobody has all the answers, but I was thinking this week, *What if the hard prayers in the Bible had been answered yes?*

What if Paul had been healed of his thorn in the flesh and had become even more impressive and had traveled even more and had learned to boast in his great strength and his great giftedness and turned the movement of the early church into a monument to human greatness?

What if Israel had become "the people of

JOHN ORTBERG

military greatness" or "the people of afflu-
ence" instead of "the people of the Book"?

Jesus asked in Gethsemane not to be cruci-
fied. What if God had said yes? What if Jesus
had been spared that cup? What if there had
been no cross, no death, no tomb, no resur-
rection, no forgiveness of sins, no outpouring
of the Holy Spirit, no birth of the church?

I don't know why some prayers get yeses
and some prayers get nos. I know the anguish
of a no when you want a yes more than you
want anything in the world. I don't know
why. I only know that in the Cross God's no
to his only Son was turned into God's yes to
every human being who ever lived.

What if I don't feel God's leading? Should I still move forward?

Some people decide that when they are facing a change, unless they get a clear direction

from God, they'll stay where they are. But why should we assume that staying is better than going? In the Bible, God hardly ever comes to someone and says, "Stay where you are." Staying as our default mode can become a strategy for comfort and safety more than faith. We decide that while we believe in God abstractly, we'd rather be in charge of our own security. We may say we believe in God, but the way we stay where we want to stay says something else.

We are staytheists.

One of the strategies people will use to try to force God to give them guidance is called "putting out a fleece," so the story this method is based on is worth a look.

God comes to a man named Gideon when he is "threshing wheat in a winepress to keep it from the Midianites" (Judges 6:11). This is a comic picture—a winepress is so small, it's like brewing tea in a thimble, and it shows how high Gideon's fear factor is.

After God tells Gideon to lead Israel into battle, Gideon says he will lay a fleece out on the threshing floor, and if there is dew on the fleece but the floor is dry, he'll know he should move forward.

And it is so.

Gideon then asks for a reverse miracle. This time he wants God to make the fleece dry but the floor dewy.

And it is so.

This has led many people to "lay out a fleece": to create a sign of some sort to confirm God's will.

Here's the problem with the fleece approach: *God had already told Gideon what to do!*

The fleece was not a sign of Gideon's faith.

The fleece was a sign of Gideon's doubt.

God was gracious enough to actually accommodate the fleece test twice. But that was a concession to Gideon's lack of faith, not a tribute to the presence of it.

A man thinks about changing jobs. He

knows of a bigger job at a better company with a higher salary. He'd really like it, but he says to himself, *I won't apply for it because I don't want to trust in myself. I'll set out a fleece: I will wait to see whether they approach me about the job without my saying anything, and that way I'll know it was God's will.*

Why would we assume that *passivity* is a greater inducement for God to reveal his will to us than *activity*? Imagine someone standing in the middle of an expressway saying, "I know all these cars are whizzing around me, but I don't want to trust in the flesh, so I'll set out a fleece—I'll just stand here, and that way if someone removes me from this traffic, I'll know it was God's will." That's just silly.

Often in life when we make a choice, we're tempted to obsess over the question of whether we chose the best option. Often this will happen most when it helps the least—when we're frustrated or depressed with our decision.

We compare the best imagined aspects of

choice B with the most exaggerated difficulties of the choice we've made: how friendly the people at place B would have been, or how much better a fit job B would have been, or what a better spouse B would have been.

We don't recognize that there is no script for how things would have gone with plan B, just as there's no script for how things will go with plan A. The biggest determinant of how things will go with plan A is whether I throw myself into this decision with great enthusiasm and prayer and hope and energy.

If I stew over what might have been, I rob myself of energy and spirit to see all the small opportunities God sets before me each day. I rob myself of precisely the spiritual assets I need to find life with God right here, right now. In other words, *often what matters most is not the decision I make but how I throw myself into executing it.* It's often better to execute an imperfect choice with your best self than the perfect choice with your wrong self.

Doris Kearns Goodwin writes that one of the reasons the American public loved Teddy Roosevelt so much was the irrepressible exuberance with which he embraced life. He never entered a door or a commitment halfheartedly. If he was in—whatever he was doing—he was all in. A contemporary of his remembers that with his great energy he even "danced just as you'd expected him to dance if you knew him. He hopped."[10]

When you face a choice and make a decision, don't limp across the threshold. Hop.

Isn't knowing "God's will for my life" reserved for spiritual giants or "professional Christians"?

One of the most crippling myths about God is that he is like some human CEO, so busy running a vast enterprise that the activities of someone as small and insignificant as me must not be the object of his attention.

In this myth's thinking, I believe there are spiritual movers and shakers out there who may have great adventures with divine doors, but I shouldn't expect that for myself. I am either not spiritual enough or not significant enough.

In the Old Testament an official named Zerubbabel was trying to get the Temple rebuilt after years of exile and neglect. He was able to manage only a meager start, which was quickly overwhelmed by opposition from without and depression from within. He felt discouraged and a failure. But through the prophet Zechariah came myth-shattering words: "Do not despise these small beginnings, for the LORD rejoices to see the work begin" (Zechariah 4:10, NLT).

A boy goes to hear a talk given by a great teacher. There is nothing special about this boy humanly speaking. He carries with him an ordinary lunch of five ordinary loaves and two ordinary fish packed by one ordinary mother. No one in that crowd looked less significant than him. And yet when the disciples were looking for food that could be shared, a thought shot through that boy's mind. He could share what he brought. He could give what he had. His small gift, in the hands of the Savior, became multiplied beyond his imagining. For two thousand years that story has been celebrated.

A widow passes by the treasury box at the Temple. She places in the box two small coins—all she has. She knows that it will be the smallest gift given, that humanly speaking it can make no difference, that from her perspective it is almost foolhardy. She could not know that one man was watching her, that he would say she actually gave more than anyone else. She could not know that her story would inspire millions of people to sacrificially give billions of dollars over the centuries.

Do not despise the day of small things. For we do not know what is small in God's eyes. Spiritual size is not measured the same way physical size is. What unit shall we use to measure love? And yet love is real, more real than anything else. When Jesus said that the widow gave *more*, it wasn't just a pretty saying; it was a spiritually accurate measurement. We just don't have that yardstick yet.

No project is so great that it doesn't need God. No project is so small that it doesn't interest God. Do not despise the day of small things. One of those Bible verses that is hard to find is "'I love grandiosity,' saith the Lord." Mother Teresa used to advise, "Don't try to do great things for God. Do small things with great love."

There was a front-page article in the *San Francisco Chronicle* about a metro transit operator named Linda Wilson-Allen.[11] She loves the people who ride her bus. She knows the regulars. She learns their names. She will wait for them if they're late and then make up the time later on her route.

A woman in her eighties named Ivy had some heavy grocery bags and was struggling with them. So Linda got out of her bus driver's seat to carry Ivy's grocery bags onto the bus. Now Ivy lets other buses pass her stop so she can ride on Linda's bus.

Linda saw a woman named Tanya in a bus shelter. She could tell Tanya was a stranger. She could tell she was lost. It was almost Thanksgiving, so Linda said to Tanya, "You're out here all by yourself. You don't know anybody. Come on over for Thanksgiving and kick it with me and the kids." Now they're friends.

The reporter who wrote the article rides Linda's bus every day. He said Linda has built such a little community of blessing on that bus that passengers offer Linda the use of their vacation homes. They bring her potted plants and floral bouquets. When people found out she likes to wear scarves to accessorize her uniforms, they started giving them as presents to Linda. One passenger upgraded her gift to a rabbit-fur collar. The article says Linda may be the most beloved bus driver since Ralph Kramden on *The Honeymooners*. (Does anybody remember old Ralph Kramden?)

Think about what a thankless task driving a bus can look like in our world: cranky passengers, engine breakdowns, traffic jams, gum on the seats. You ask yourself, *How does she have this attitude?* "Her mood is set at 2:30 a.m. when she gets down on her knees to pray for 30 minutes," the *Chronicle* said. "'There is a lot to talk about with the Lord,' says Wilson-Allen, a member of Glad Tidings Church in Hayward."

When she gets to the end of her line, she always says, "That's all. I love you. Take care." Have you ever had a bus driver tell you, "I love you"? People wonder, *Where can I find the Kingdom of God?* I will tell you where. You can find it on the #45 bus riding through

San Francisco. People wonder, *Where can I find the church?* Behind the wheel of a metro transit vehicle.

Too often in thinking about God's will, we look for *other* circumstances. The way to start is by asking about God's will for me not there and then but here and now. Dallas Willard writes:

> We must accept the circumstances we constantly find ourselves in as the place of God's kingdom and blessing. God has yet to bless anyone except where they actually are, and if we faithlessly discard situation after situation, moment after moment, as not being "right," we will simply have no place to receive his kingdom into our life. For those situations and moments *are* our life.
>
> Our life presents itself to us as a series of tasks. Our more serious challenges are *trials*, even *tribulations*. . . . Just listen to how people carry on! For some of

us the first tribulation of the day is just getting up. And then there is caring for ourselves. Then the commute. Then work and other people. But knowledge of the kingdom puts us in position to welcome all of these.[12]

Furthermore, God can speak to anyone he wants, and it does not mean that person has grounds for pride. One of the most colorful stories in the Old Testament involves a prophet named Balaam. Israel's enemies want him to practice "divination"—to use stars or palms or crystal balls to predict the future so they can defeat Israel.

God sends an angel to block Balaam's way. Balaam cannot see the angel, but his donkey can and turns aside from the road. When Balaam beats his donkey, "the LORD opened the donkey's mouth, and it said to Balaam, 'What have I done to you to make you beat me these three times? . . . Am I not your own donkey, which you have always ridden, to this day? Have I been in the habit of doing this to you?'" (Numbers 22:28, 30).

"No," Balaam admits.

I love that Balaam gets out-argued by his donkey.

But Balaam's donkey, even though God spoke through it, was still just a donkey.

Can I want something so badly that God has to give it to me?

Often we want to do something so badly that we're able to convince ourselves that God is telling us to do it. The classic example is a hungry car driver who suddenly spots a donut shop. *This must be a gift from heaven*, he thinks. *But I will submit to God. If there is an open parking spot in front of the donut shop, then I'll know it's God's will for me to have a donut.*

Sure enough, the sixth time he drives around the block, there's an open parking spot.

Should I date somebody? If I should, who should it be? How do I know if we should get married, if she is "the one"? What do I do if *I* know she's the one and *God* knows she's the one, but she hasn't gotten the word yet? What school should I go to? What should I choose as a major? What's the right career track for me to be on? What job should I take? Where should I live? Which house should I buy?

Does God want me to persevere in this difficult situation because I'm supposed to grow? Or does he want me to leave it because, after all, he wants me to be happy?

From ancient times on, human beings have wanted to consult supernaturally authoritative sources to know the future and know which choice to make. They have read palms and tea leaves and stars and animal entrails. They have consulted oracles and tarot cards and Ouija boards. They have drawn straws and cast lots.

To this day such practices persist despite

certain logical inconsistencies. People call the Psychic Friends hotline—if they're psychic friends, shouldn't they call *you*? If you're going to see a psychic, shouldn't appointments be unnecessary? I heard about one man who said he had almost had a psychic girlfriend, but she broke up with him before he met her.

The faith of Israel was quite intolerant of these practices—not just because they don't work but because of the critical difference between faith and magic. In fact, there's a weird and fascinating story about King Saul that helps us understand the difference.

Saul has rejected God's leadership of his life. He has chosen the door of power, jealousy, deception, and ego. The Philistines are threatening war. Saul is desperate to know what to do, so he suddenly seeks "God's will for his life"—should he fight the Philistines or not?

But Saul doesn't really want "God's will." He doesn't want to repent, humble himself, confess his wrongdoings, or make restoration.

He just wants the success of his own agenda. So heaven is silent. God cannot answer Saul's request in any way that would be truly helpful to Saul.

Saul can't get a response to his prayer, so he consults a medium in Endor and asks her to summon the dead prophet Samuel. (Necromancy—seeking to discern the future by consulting the dead—is one of the oldest forms of divination.)

Samuel appears and asks Saul rather testily what he wants. Saul answers, "I am in great distress, for the Philistines are warring against me, and God has turned away from me and answers me no more, either by prophets or by dreams; so I have summoned you to tell me what I should do" (1 Samuel 28:15, NRSV).

What is driving Saul (and often drives us) is given away in the first phrase: "I am in great distress." Making decisions is stressful. And sometimes I'm not looking for "God's

will" so much as a guarantee of future out-
comes that will take the responsibility of decision off my shoulders. God *has to* tell me
what to do, for "I am in great distress."

Samuel does not give Saul the advice Saul
is looking for. Instead Samuel repeats the
moral and spiritual judgment that could save
Saul but that Saul has already rejected.

There is a huge difference between faith,
on the one hand, and magic or superstition
on the other. In superstition, I seek to use
some supernatural force to accomplish my
own agenda. Martin Buber said, "Magic desires to obtain its effects without entering
into relation, and practices its tricks in the
void."[13] We are tempted to use superstition
to be spared anxiety, or to avoid blame for
our own wrongdoing, or to bail us out of
trouble, or to seek inside information to get
what we want. Magic gives us the illusion of
knowledge when none really exists. Groucho
Marx is supposed to have said, "If a black cat

crosses your path, it signifies that the animal is going somewhere."

Superstition seeks to use the supernatural for my purposes; faith seeks to surrender to God's purposes. Faith teaches us that there is a Person behind the universe, and that Person responds to communication, just as all persons do. Prayer is the primary way we communicate with God, and that's why prayer is so closely associated with seeking and discerning God's will.

But in the actual practice of our faith, superstition is as great a temptation for us as it was for Saul.

A man was convinced that it was God's will that one particular woman was his "soul mate." There was a particular song that he associated with her, and he decided that if, when he turned on the radio, that song was playing, it would be a sign from God that she in fact was "the one." The song was playing.

She was not "the one." In fact, she considered

his behavior closer to stalking than to courting. A good rule of thumb is that if the person you think is "the one" considers you to be a stalker, he or she may not be "the one."

In fact, "soul mate" is not actually a biblical term. There was a Greek myth that human beings were originally both male and female who somewhere along the line got ripped in half, and therefore we spend our lives looking for our "other half," or soul mate. But that's not in the Bible. And if I'm asking, "God, is this the one?" I'm missing the opportunity to learn what comes when I ask, "God, make me wise."

In the Bible, the prophet Isaiah notes the futility of superstition in pursuing the will of God:

All the counsel you have received has only worn you out! Let your astrologers come forward, those stargazers who make predictions month by month, let them save you from what is coming upon you. Surely they are like stubble; the fire will burn them up. They cannot even save themselves from the power of the flame. . . . All of them go on in their error; there is not one that can save you. (Isaiah 47:13-15)

The book of Deuteronomy notes that such superstition is not just futile, it's forbidden:

Let no one be found among you who sacrifices their son or daughter in the fire, who practices divination or sorcery, interprets omens, . . . or who is a medium or spiritist or who consults the dead. (Deuteronomy 18:10-11)

The reason such practices were forbidden is that they are an attempt to *use* the divine without *being accountable to* the divine. They approach spiritual power as something we might be able to use for selfish advantage, and they disconnect it from the claims of justice and love that lie at the heart of God's will for his creation.

Sometimes it works like this: a person says "I *must* have that relationship or that possession or that job. When I think of obtaining it, I feel peace; when I think of losing it, I lose peace. God wants me to have peace; therefore, this object of my desire must be God's will for my life." Maybe. But maybe God's will is for my sense of peace to be founded on firmer ground.

Maybe I need to quit circling the donut shop.

How do I learn to recognize God's voice?

Jesus teaches in John 10,

> The one who enters by the gate is the shepherd of the sheep. The gatekeeper

opens the gate for him, and the *sheep listen to his voice. . . . His sheep follow him because they know his voice.* But they will never follow a stranger; in fact, they will run away from him because *they do not recognize a stranger's voice.* (verses 2-5, emphasis mine)

But what does it mean to hear the shepherd's voice?

Some people seem to "hear God's voice" all the time. They may often sense or talk about his guidance in their lives. Other people may be equally devout but never have a sense that they are "hearing God's voice." They may feel that their spiritual lives are less vital, or they may wonder if those who claim to hear God's voice are being presumptuous or faking something.

Some people are deeply skeptical of such claims—although, of course, it's not really more incredible to think that God can speak than that God can listen. Comedian Lily Tomlin asked, "Why is it that when we talk to God, it's called 'prayer,' but when God talks to us, it's called 'schizophrenia?'"

Some believe that a claim to hear God's voice involves a level of mysticism that goes beyond what the Bible teaches. On the other hand, Frank Laubach defines a mystic as someone who believes that when you talk to God, God talks back.

Perhaps the simplest way to think about hearing God's voice is to consider communication in general. The best definition of communication is simply *guiding thoughts*.[14] When a person speaks, the listener has thoughts that would otherwise not occur to her. Because we are finite, we have to use finite means to guide each other's thoughts. So we speak words by making sounds, or we write words by using letters. Because you are reading these words, you are having thoughts right now (hopefully!) that you would not be having otherwise.

God also "guides thoughts." We see this happening often in stories in the Bible. However, since God is infinite, he is able to guide or plant or cause a thought to occur in our minds without using finite means at all.

One of the consequences of this is that God might be guiding a particular line of thought in my mind without my being aware of it.

We see this in the Bible in the story of a young boy named Samuel. Samuel is living in the Tabernacle—the place above all other places in Israel that represents God's desire to live in interactive friendship with human beings.

At night Samuel hears his name being called. He does not know how to respond; the text says, "In those days the word of the LORD was rare; there were not many visions" (1 Samuel 3:1). Three times the Lord calls his name; three times Samuel runs to Eli, thinking the voice is his. In a telling aside the writer says, "Now Samuel did not yet know the LORD: The word of the LORD had not yet been revealed to him" (1 Samuel 3:7). In other words, God is speaking to Samuel, and Samuel is hearing, but he does not yet recognize that it is God.

After the third time Eli—who has greater spiritual experience and perhaps is getting a little sleepy—tells Samuel to go back to bed and that if he hears the voice again, he should say, "Speak, for your servant is listening" (1 Samuel 3:10). Samuel does, and this is the beginning of a rich interactive spiritual relationship in which "the LORD was with Samuel as he grew up, and he let none of Samuel's words fall to the ground. . . . He revealed himself to Samuel through his word" (1 Samuel 3:19, 21).

Here we see what might be called the "ministry of Eli." Samuel needed someone else to help him consider that God might be speaking to him. Samuel was young, and "in

those days the word of the LORD was rare"—
there were many reasons why Samuel might
doubt. Just as there are for us.

But Eli's guidance was instructive. "Speak,
Lord, for your servant is listening." He in-
structs Samuel to be open to the possibility that God is addressing him. And he tells
Samuel that the right posture for listening to
God is as a servant. A servant is humble—the
idea that God might be guiding us is never
grounds for pride. And a servant is ready to
carry out the master's direction. Learning to
recognize the voice of God is less often a matter of remarkable discernment or spiritual
antennae than it is simple obedience.

- A cranky neighbor leaves an irritable
  voicemail, and you are tempted to hold
  a grudge, but then the "word of the
  Lord" speaks: "Love your neighbor."
- You're tempted to spend your work
  bonus on a luxury vacation, and then

the "word of the Lord" speaks: "Store up for yourself treasure in heaven."

- You're on a crowded expressway during rush hour when someone wants to pull in front of you. You're tempted to respond with frustration and impatience when the "word of the Lord" speaks (not "Get behind me, Satan!")—"Do to others what you would have others do to you."

The main way we learn to recognize God's voice in situations where we're not sure what to do is by obeying him in situations where his will is clear.

Much as with people—we learn to recognize someone's voice by experience. When I know someone well, I will know their voice because it has a certain tone and a certain character that is familiar to me.

"Voice recognition" is a learned skill, and it's something we're able to do even though we might not be able to describe how we've done it. Primarily it comes by experience. A little child hears his or her mother speaking and soon is able to pick her voice out over a thousand others. Researchers talk about the ability to recognize someone's "acoustic identity."

God has built this capacity into us. In fact, even in the animal kingdom a baby penguin will be able to pick its mother's voice out in a colony that may contain a million penguins![15]

When good friends call you on the phone, immediately you "know their voice." How? Mainly by experience. Over time, you recognize the sound of their voice. It has a certain tone and quality. Plus, you know that there are certain things that your friend is likely to say to you and other things they would not. It is the combination of tone and content that lets us learn someone's voice.

And it's the same with the voice of God.

There are certain things God will not say. He won't say:

- "Be anxious"; or
- "Think only about yourself"; or
- "You might as well give up in despair."

I might be tempted to say those things to myself. But if I hear those thoughts, I can be confident they are not from God.

Developing the ability to be guided by God is more about consistent obedience than about spectacular discernment.

But I must cultivate the habit of listening. This means making the time and space for reflection. It requires that I stop talking every now and again and get away from noise and screens and stimulation. It means silence. In George Bernard Shaw's play about Joan of Arc, Joan is on trial before the weak and easily frustrated King Charles. Joan explains the inspiration for her extraordinary actions: "I hear voices telling me what to do. They come from God."

The exasperated king says, "Oh, your voices. . . . Why don't the voices come to me? I am king, not you."

Joan answers, "They do come to you; but you do not hear them. You have not sat in the field in the evening listening for them. . . . If you prayed from your heart, and listened . . . you would hear the voices as well as I do."

Final thought . . .

"'I know the plans I have for you,' declares the LORD."

What a wonderful promise.

Not a burden.

Not a guessing game.

No more pressure.

No more paralysis.

It's a promise that all God's will—the bits

we know and the bits we don't—is bent toward our flourishing in his care.

It's an invitation to grow in wisdom, surrender, love, and grace. You can respond to the invitation today. Now.

It's your decision.

ENDNOTES

1. Andy Chan, "Called to the Future," manuscript accepted for publication in *Theology, News & Notes* (Pasadena, CA: Fuller Theological Seminary, 2014).
2. Sheena Iyengar, "How to Make Choosing Easier," TED talk, November 2011, http://www.ted.com /talks/sheena_iyengar_choosing_what_to_choose.
3. Frederick Buechner, *The Sacred Journey* (New York: HarperCollins, 1982), 104.
4. Dallas Willard, personal communication with the author.
5. Archibald MacLeish, quoted in Sheena Iyengar, *The Art of Choosing* (New York: Hachette, 2010), xvii.
6. Dr. Seuss, *Oh, the Places You'll Go!* (New York: Random House, 1990), 25.
7. Barry Schwartz, "The Paradox of Choice," TED talk, July 2005, http://www.ted.com/talks/barry_schwartz _on_the_paradox_of_choice.
8. Chip Heath and Dan Heath, *Decisive* (New York: Random House, 2013), 10.

9. This story is found in Parker J. Palmer, *Let Your Life Speak: Listening for the Voice of Vocation* (San Francisco: Jossey-Bass, 2000), 44–46.

10. Doris Kearns Goodwin, *The Bully Pulpit* (New York: Simon & Schuster, 2013), 44.

11. Sam Whiting, "Muni Driver Will Make New Friends, Keep the Old," *San Francisco Chronicle*, September 8, 2013, http://www.sfchronicle.com/bayarea/article /Muni-driver-will-make-new-friends-keep-the-old -4797537.php#/0.

12. Dallas Willard, *The Divine Conspiracy* (New York: HarperCollins, 1998), 348–349.

13. Quoted in Dallas Willard, *Hearing God* (Downers Grove, IL: InterVarsity Press, 2012), 180.

14. See Willard, *Hearing God.*

15. Karine Lou Matignon, *The Emotional Life of Animals* (Old Saybrook, CT: Konecky & Konecky LLC, 2006), 51.

NOTES

NOTES

NOTES

NOTES